Shack Blessings

A Therapist's Guide To Understanding Our Inner Shack

Lola Carlile, Ph.D.
Art Therapy Counselor/Educator

Shack Blessings

A therapist's guide to understanding our inner shack

Masabi Press
PO Box 2663
Salem, OR 97308
www.masabi.org

Text copyright Lola Carlile, Ph.D.

All rights reserved. No part of this publication may be reproduced, stored in a retrieval system, or transmitted in any form or by any means, electrical, mechanical, photocopying, recording, or otherwise, whether for commercial, public, or private use without the prior written permission of the publisher.

Layout design by Mosher Multimedia.

Copyright 2017

ISBN:
978-1544068701

Subjects: Therapy, art, women's studies, spiritual, philosophy, self help

The Shack to the Rescue

I had been battling anxiety and depression for quite a while when my friend invited me to go listen to a guy who wrote a book about the Trinity. She hadn't read it, but heard it was a wonderful read and she urged me to read it before we went to the talk. I wasn't much interested, as I had never heard of the book, "The Shack," or the author, but, since she was so enthusiastic, and being a good friend, I begrudgingly took the book from her to read, and when I started, I could not put it down. I emailed her immediately and told her not to read it, as it was about someone's child dying, or so I thought. It was much more, (this friend's 18-year old daughter had been kidnapped and murdered in the capital of Oregon a few years back).

After reading the book, I was hooked, hyped, and happy to share with anyone I met, the beautiful message contained in those pages of a book I would never forget.

In this much beloved book, Mack never forgot about the tragedy. If you have not read this book, I hope you do, so I won't add too many spoilers. Mack tried suppressing the guilt, the fear, and anger, and the deepest hurt of all, yet it was always with him, ready to spring out and choke him with its intensity. As the unwanted weed spreads its seed and conquers all other plant life, those strongest of weeds sprout in the most unlikely places - so it was that Mack found those emotions of negativity.

We often allow the weeds of disquiet and discontent to roam through our souls and minds. We sometimes forget that we can either allow those feelings to guide and rule us, or we can cast them aside, replacing them with positive and healing thoughts. It is really our choice.

This book is written for you to reflect, occasionally genuflect, and interact, making a positive shift in your perceptions and interactions with life. It is a time to heal your soul and prepare your life for joy, contentment, and peace.

Searching

I am constantly amazed when folks say they haven't read "*The Shack*." For me, it was a pivotal time in my relationship with the supernatural. But, for some, "*The Shack*" appears to have managed to inspire, irritate or infuriate its readers, sometimes with a combination of such reactions.

Why all the fuss? Isn't it "just a novel?" Whatever your reaction to the book, it offers us all an opportunity to open up conversations about God, suffering and a host of related topics.

What is your understanding of relationships? Are you one of those who think a good relationship must be a 50/50 partnership? How does that work?

Trust was a big deal to Mack. He wasn't sure he trusted his God and what he saw in the shack truly amazed him. I guess it is okay not to trust in a relationship, but one side has to give that unfettered and completely unconditional love.

I might be able to use that with a few people I am trying to love in my life, but it is not easy. This book illustrates how living lovingly can be done. Paul's amazing book keeps teaching us life's lessons a bit at a time.

Not only is he sharing his life's story, Paul is also available to others through conferences and emails. Paul does a wonderful job of making the supernatural real and relevant in this chaotic world.

What are you searching for? What will it take for you to find it? Do you even know? On the next page, draw a timeline for when you first remember searching for happiness, God, or peace. Along the way, write or draw the impediments or supports that helped you get to where you are today.

Reflection

Depression and Fear

The cold kept bringing Mack back into focus. Wintertime brings a slew of problems, with just being plain ole' cold as one of them. Yes, Mack knew he had the odd letter somewhere. Meet who? And why? Would anyone in his right mind actually go back to that blasted place and relive those nightmares? Why would Mack even consider it? Sometimes we revisit our past negativity and invite it into our souls. And sometimes those past horrors have a way of dissipating and disappearing. Surely, Mack was afraid. Aren't we all?

We all have fears. Sometimes we just try to bury them in the myriad thoughts in our mind. If we don't think about them, they will disappear, correct? Wrong.

Fears are common to mankind. Ever since caveman days, to be honest. We are wired to sense danger. We are wired to react by either fleeing or fighting. Think of the last time you were afraid. Was it the time you were traveling in the dark and your car broke down? Think back to how you felt. It might not be this exact situation, but think of one.

Visualize yourself in that situation. Was your heart beating fast? Were you feeling faint? Did you want to hide? Did you witness others slow down and maybe even stop? Did you want to protect yourself from imaginary or real danger? What parts of your brain were on high alert?

You can make a difference. You can decide how to react when placed in a threatening situation. You must first, though, realize that you have this choice. You can either face these strong feelings, sublimate them for a while, or never deal with them.

What are you afraid of? Draw your fears and confront them on the next page. What have you to lose? Come to grips that you cannot control thoughts or others, but you CAN control how you react to them. Later on in this book you will find out strategies that will help; however, it will take considerable work on your part to make it part of your personality. It takes a lot of perseverance and hard work. But you can do it!

Reflection

Legacy

As I think back on Paul's journey writing **The Shack**, I marvel that a man who was so down and out had the energy to think of his children and the desire to create a legacy for them. He pulled himself out of the mire and wrote from his heart. His actions inspire millions to understand the true meaning of our very existence. If you do not know the story of Wm. Paul Young, the short of it is that he did not have resources for gifts for Christmas one year. He was down and out as they say, so he wrote a book for his children and friends and found some compassionate soul to print the story at the local copy store. The rest of the story is amazing - he went from a self-published author to a world-renowned artist published in many other countries.

Do you allow your past journeys into hell create a better you in the now?

Can you write your story for your descendants? Will they be able to understand who they are based on your story? Like the old Nike slogan said, *just do it*!

My mother was the daughter of a Romanian Roman Catholic priest in the 1940s. Those of you who know, Roman Catholic priests are not allowed to get married. That sin he committed, according to the church, had him excommunicated from the church. As I grew up, I noticed he had an altar on a table in his bedroom. He often blessed us as did the priest. I simply thought all old European men did this. He prayed the rosary every evening.

During his twilight years, he was welcomed back to the church, although I felt he was always in it. Those stories help me in my daily life. He persevered. He was a good man whom I never heard raise his voice. He delighted in teaching me Latin and math when I visited. He spoke more than ten languages. I feel his legacy is one that I honor and try to somehow emulate.

On this page, reflect on how you conquer your demons, no matter how big or small. Do so in art, poetry, photos, or just journaling. The choice is yours. Who has inspired you?

Reflection

Excuses and Wrongs

Mack made all sorts of excuses, and the more he thought about that missive that appeared one day in his mailbox with no stamp or return address, the more exacerbated his problems became. Why, he even fell on the ice and cut himself up pretty badly. Just trying to ignore God doesn't really work. He's patient even if we are not.

Mack dismissed the letter for he really didn't understand who it could really be from. It didn't even have a stamp on it and no return address. Do we get messages and not understand them as well in our lives?

Mack didn't know who the missive was from…could it be from God? Nah. Sometimes we don't recognize when God is talking to us. How can we be sure? Will we go to meet Him, if only out of curiosity?

What sorts of messages do we send out both electronically and in person? Do we just spout off anything that comes to mind (a personal habit I have tried to eradicate) or do we think about what should be said?

On the next page write a letter to someone who has wronged you or to someone you have wronged. Let the words flow from your heart. Then either rip it out and destroy it or keep it in this book to remember – we can forgive if only to allow ourselves to feel the elation of lifting heaviness from our heart.

Reflection

Dealing with Death

Death is so hard to deal with, especially if it is your own child. And then there is the guilt. How does one live with that? Only if, should have, could have....blaming. Mack had a lot on his plate and in that shack he learned more about himself than he could ever have learned on his own.

Is there a nagging thought or heaviness in your heart about someone's passing through this amazing journey we call life? How do you deal with the aftermath of death?

Some folks talk about it a lot to a lot of people. Some draw or make art to honor the individual who has passed. Others write. I wrote a book called, **Grandma's Shindig – A Grandma's Journey to Heaven**, to honor my mother. Still others bring flowers to the grave.

Once you become proactive about the individual, your pain lessens. Mind you I did not say it disappears. The pain will always be there, but can be a pain that gives us strength and peace as well.

Cultural mores and standards dictate how we deal with life and death. In Western culture, we quickly deliver the deceased to the mortuary and sometimes even reduce the individual to ashes. Not so morbid that way, some say. More environmentally aware, others tout. How are we to deal with this loss?

Draw what that feels like – if you are uncomfortable with drawing, you can scribble, paint abstract lines, or find pictures or photos to represent your feelings....loneliness, refuge, depression, unthinkable loss....what other words could you use?

Reflection

Fear and Memories

Mack was afraid to go into the shack. He thought only horrid memories would meet him, but he was pleasantly surprised. The light shone brightly and nature opened up her beauteous colors for him.

We think of fall as a prelude to an end, but perhaps it is the culmination of our angst and pitfalls all forgiven and dressed in glory. Deep breath. Close your eyes and let the beauty permeate your soul.

I read somewhere that if you live in the past or future, you will not be experiencing the present and the present is all we are assured of and all we can control, if control is even possible. Yes, control of how we perceive the present is definitely something we can accomplish.

Take a mind trip. Look around you. Find three things that are pleasing in your sight. Glance at them and think of the qualities that make those things pleasing. Color? Shape? Perhaps the item is a gift from someone special. Keep gazing at your environment. Think positively. Take a deep breath and exhale slowly. Life is beautiful. We just only have to look around.

On the next page, find beautiful colors in your world at your favorite season. Draw or paint them. Allow your eyes to gaze upon their diversity and intensity.

Reflection

Heaven and the Trinity

The love, freedom, and acceptance in the Trinity as portrayed in **The Shack** amazes and refreshes our sensibilities. Three diverse, yet three very loving individuals work together to make Nirvana appealing and quite understanding.

Growing up, most of us had thoughts of Heaven as a place in the clouds where everyone wore angel wings and played harps and eventually that serene scene became unbelievable. And boring. Just being honest here. It finally came to the point when I heard others say, "Oh, Uncle Joe is up there playing dominoes with Grandma," that I started losing my belief in a heaven. I just knew that was not true. Or is it?

I know that my faith has to change from that of a simple child to a faith of an adult. I don't believe any of us truly knows for sure what heaven is like. I know we think we know. When I try to visualize it, I become frustrated, so have just decided I will find out eventually!

At this point, I think of the caveman. What would he think if he saw rockets, or cell phones, or even microwaves? I don't think many cavemen even thought or dreamt about those things. They simply could not comprehend. So that is how I come to terms with not understanding. While heaven may not be comprehensible to me now, its truth and beauty will be revealed to me in time. I must just be patient.

What is your concept of heaven? Does the fog disguise your mind?

Reflection

Trust

Trust is the fruit of a relationship in which you know you are loved.

Relationships are never about power, and one way to avoid the desire to exert power over someone or something is to choose to limit oneself - to serve. In serving, one is thinking about others instead of self. Well said, Papa! To be sure, giving of oneself keeps one from becoming powerful.

Forgiveness does not establish relationship. When you forgive someone you certainly release them from judgment, but without true change, no real relationship can be established.

Many people go through life with biases, likes, dislikes, and all the baggage that goes with intense emotions. Some do not realize they do have a choice. One does not have to let others dictate how we feel. We can choose to acknowledge evil, anger, and negativity, but we can also choose to not allow that to affect our spirit and souls.

We have the choice to be happy, to enjoy life, and to have a soul filled with joy. When we reach this state, we have reached what some term Nirvana. The more we practice our craft of forgiving and accepting and loving, the more we will feel we have reached the peace our souls long for.

In this chapter's photo, the wild-flowers are blooming. We can trust they will bloom season after season. So, too, our souls should bloom with brilliance and beauty.

On the next page, draw or cut out from a magazine or place a photo of something that gives you pleasure. Focus on it. Look at the shapes, the colors, and take a deep breath. You are indeed being in the moment.

Reflection

Appearances Can Be Deceiving

You cannot produce trust just like you cannot 'do' humility. It either is or is not. Trust is the fruit of a relationship in which you know you are loved. This bears repeating from the last chapter because it is so essential to understand.

It's a matter of perspective. The same shack. The same camera. The same photographer, yet both photos are different and evoke a deep sense of wonder in one and mystery in the other. What is on your outside? What do people see of the real you? Or are you simply masking yourself to appeal to the masses?

Both photos are real. But each one reveals something quite different. One allows the viewer to become close and personal. The other image simply beckons one to look at generalities.

What do you want others to see or not see about you? Do you have a true awareness of the real you? Or have you hidden yourself so deeply you do not even recognize who you truly are?

Sometimes past experiences create a vacuum in us and we fill that space with trite and shallow meaning in order to close the hole. But the real pain and anguish simply is pushed deeper down inside of us. It is still there and we have to deal with it in order to create harmony within our spirits.

Draw or find photos of your home or apartment. What things happen inside that make you grow, wonder, and become a better human being?

Reflection

Journey to the Unknown

As we know, Mack received an invitation to return to the shack, yet he wasn't even sure who it was from. He couldn't exactly throw it away, but at the same time, he tried to ignore it. He fought it with all he had. He stashed it in his pocket; and tried to return to the house on his icy driveway. He made it to the house with considerable difficulty. His journey outside was not what he expected.

Glancing at our picture on this page, we think that surely a shack could be in this picture, but the flora has grown up so much around it, that it is invisible to our eye. It is still there and needs tending. Our problems still exist, but the more we pretend they do not exist, the more our inner worries grow.

What in your life has caused you to cast aside some action, invitation, or happening simply because you didn't know the source or were unsure of what might happen?

Sometimes we worry about things we cannot control. Money woes can consume the space in our minds at one time or another in our life. The more we ignore those worries, the more worried we get. It is only when we take action that our life becomes freer and more peaceful.

Worrying about the past creates depression, and worry about the future only serves to make us more anxious. We must be in the moment. So, how do we take these worries and convert them to peaceful and meaningful thoughts?

Create a container for your worries. Remember Mack thrust his letter into his pocket. He knew it was there. You are not getting rid of your worries; you are prioritizing them.

Take a moment and draw a receptacle below. Anything that holds something. Then write inside that receptacle things you worry about that you are going to work on later. Right now you are going to be in the moment. Enjoy making your receptacle. It can even be a 3-D product. It does not have to be on this page. Simply write about what you make or photograph it. After you are finished, put those worries in it, close the container (your safe place) and take a deep breath.

Reflection

Relationships

God tells Mack, *"We are not in a chain of command, we are in a circle of relationship."* How amazing is that? In order to flourish and grow in this life, we must be aware of relationships and grow them, so to speak. If we spend the majority of our waking moments thinking about our needs and how others might or should fulfill them, we are missing out on the purpose of life. Is there someone in your life whom you need to nurture your relationship with? Who might that be? What are you doing that is fostering a positive relationship and what could you do to create a more enduring and loving relationship?

Sometimes we need to shine a light on our shack so that all who enter into our lives are able to experience a brighter and clearly more understandable relationship. *What lights can you install in your life?*

Reflection

Looking Within

Messy, overgrown weeds, and debris can turn a place of rest to a thorn in one's life. Mack is told that, "*honesty can be messy*." Is there some truth in thinking that sometimes honesty can be just mean? An old adage says something like, "If you can't say anything nice, don't say anything at all."

Who gave us the responsibility of pointing out other folks' faults? Should we not tidy and organize our own lives before we attempt to cleanse others?

When are times we must be honest? Parents, counselors, teachers, and all those who guide others need to remember to be kind, yet honest. I grew up in the M&M generation of teachers. Every time a kid did something, we gave that child an M&M. Pretty soon kids were asking for the M&Ms. We didn't realize that we were creating a dependent class. One that would not work unless we gave rewards. I guess some of us missed the psychology class where we were supposed to begin limiting and phasing out the rewards so that the responses would be unconditioned responses eventually. I don't know why, but we kept giving those M&Ms. Thankfully, those students did not suffer, as we probably ran out of the candy or got tired of giving them and moved on to something different. Yes, I know. We said, "Good job. Nice! Wonderful!" Yes, we learned to change our behavior a little at a time. How has your honesty served you?

I think we were afraid we would hurt the children if we gave them constructive criticism. Later on, life changed and all kids were winners in sports. Everyone got a trophy. Competition was frowned on. There were no scores in children's sports. Hopefully, we all have learned that one must be honest with oneself and with others. There is just a kind way to do so.

Write some things you feel you need to change in your own life – attitudes, expectations, or actions. Write those or draw them and create a plan to alleviate your life of those burdens.

Reflection

Rules or Higher Love

In this day and age, much anger and dissent permeates our culture. Can you imagine being able to converse with God about religion and politics? His statement to Mack was, *"So no, I'm not too big on religion, and not very fond of politics or economics either, and why should I be? They are the man-created trinity of terrors that ravages the earth and deceives those I care about. What mental turmoil and anxiety does any human face that is not related to one of those three?"*

How refreshing to realize that organized religion is not high on God's list of priorities. If God is love and we love one another, as well as ourselves, aren't we becoming like God? When we make man-made rules more important than the simple rules given by our God, then we simply are ignoring the truth. God IS love. We must love first and foremost.

We can't isolate ourselves on a cliff somewhere in the wilderness hoping to learn about the world. We need one another. We need relationships. We need to love and be loved. Mack is told, *"Trust is the fruit of a relationship in which you know you are loved."*

I was taught that God is love and if I love myself, then am I not being godlike? I don't mean to be blasphemous. It's just that it fits if we are to follow the tenets of the Lord, we can't just pick and choose what we want to do. We must give with our whole heart, soul, and mind.

Compile a list of those you love and another one of those you do not love. How can you merge the two lists into one? What can you do to make this happen? Do you have trust?

Reflection

God's Will

Mack is told, *"Just because I work incredible good out of unspeakable tragedies doesn't mean I orchestrate the tragedies. Don't ever assume that my using something means I caused it or that I need it to accomplish my purposes."*

How many times do you hear, "Oh, it is God's will?" And then the naysayers complain about a cruel and unjust God. Perhaps this quote is right – we are given free will. We humans can make decisions. Those decisions have consequences. What about the horrible tragedies that occur? Is it not just a consequence of actions somewhere? Perhaps we should stop blaming others for our own misfortunes. Picking a better place to build one's shack makes more sense than blaming the hurricane for blowing it down. We need to be sure our inner shack is stable.

People lose their religion over tragedies. They exclaim, "I don't love or believe in God anymore because he allowed my son to die." It is definitely more difficult for some to understand the nuances of life. Yes, life can be unfair. It can be cruel. But the fact of the matter is we have choices. We can believe the negativity surrounding events or we can be hopeful and look to our spiritual lives to heal us.

How have you built your character, your inner shack? Have you created a strong, purposeful way to act? Or have you just thrown together an inner belief system ready to fall with the slightest provocation?

Reflection

Healing Tears

During a strong downpour, we watch from our inner haven. We know the rain purifies, nurtures, and encourages beauty to flourish. We need the purging at times. So when it says in **The Shack**, *"Don't ever discount the wonder of your tears. They can be healing waters and a stream of joy. Sometimes they are the best words the heart can speak,"* we know that a good cry sometimes is the cleansing our inner spirit requires.

The other day I was feeling ill and as I lay in bed, I began to think of my dear mother. She has been gone for almost a decade. Before I knew it, I was crying my heart out, missing her more than I can say. I felt myself spiraling and realized that as a child, my mother was of such comfort to me, and now, as an adult, I needed that comforting. I recovered quickly and thanked her for being my mom, for I do know her spirit is aware of me even today.

Think of the sound of the rain. The pelting unrelenting streams of water falling or the gentle pitter patter of a soft rain. When was the last time you cried? What was it about? How did you feel afterwards?

Reflection

Forgiveness

Forgiveness is difficult. Most of us have carried a grudge in our hearts, sometimes for decades. Baggage such as this only serves to harden our hearts, increase our burden of stress and anxiety, but it takes away precious time and space for our own happiness.

"Forgiveness does not excuse anything... You may have to declare your forgiveness a hundred times the first day and the second day, but the third day will be less and each day after, until one day you will realize that you have forgiven completely."

What an astute comment, "Forgiveness doesn't excuse anything." If someone wrongs you, you are able to forgive them and to allow their judgment to be someone else's problem. It is no longer your problem. It does not have to complicate your life. Doing so creates a total sense of freedom within.

So, are you holding on to some ancient grudge? Start today to let it go. Write or draw this grudge on the next page. Remember to take deep breaths and start the healing process. Send your thoughts to a beautiful sunset. The anger, the pain, and the anguish you have experienced will be sent to the sunset of this relationship.

A new dawn will appear tomorrow and you will be the recipient of healing and the joy you have been denying yourself. Remember, it is not easy, and you may have to repeat this forgiveness act countless times until it finally disappears from the horizon. Just as the sun sets daily, so you will have to continually purge your soul of your pain.

For years I carried a burden of hurt from an individual. That person was cruel, lied, and was generally a bad man. I avoided him and nurtured my hurt. I felt like a victim. I may have even perseverated about the incidents that occurred decades ago. It was only when I finally told myself it was not my problem, and it was then I realized I didn't own the hurt anymore. I didn't feel the pain. It was gone. That doesn't mean he was exonerated. It's just that his actions are no longer my concern. Others will judge and sentence him. I no longer am in that picture. The actual physical relief I felt when I truly forgave this man is unimaginable. I could breathe once again without pain.

Reflection

Submission

"Submission is not about authority and it is not obedience."

We often hear that to be religious one must be submissive. Feminist alert! We all know those who deride the term submissive. To them submissive means we have lost ourselves. But to be truly submissive to God, to the universe, means that we finally admit to ourselves that there are greater forces than our humble selves. We acknowledge humbly that we do not know everything and we finally agree that we will continue to search for truth, but it is not as elusive as one might have thought. Truth is in love and love is everywhere. Sometimes we are looking too far away for what is inside of us.

Our path is not that difficult. We just need to be aware, to be focused, and we will find wonders beyond our best expectations.

What have you been struggling with in your heart? Have you allowed pride to keep you from finding love and peace? Has stubbornness kept you from releasing true peace and happiness within?

"Not at all," smiled Jesus as he reached for the door handle to the shop. *"Most roads don't lead anywhere. What it does mean is that I will travel any road to find you."*

People get hung up on trivialities and even some Christians will proudly state that the only way to go to heaven is through Jesus Christ. Yes, most Christians believe that, but there is a deep dark secret most do not truly know. If Christ came to save all of us, how in the world would he punish those who are not baptized? What if he doesn't? What if there are other forms of "baptism?"

Is there a case for non-Christians going to heaven? Are there multiple paths to heaven? Whether you believe that redemption is available to others or not is irrelevant. What is important is that you stop judging others and cleanse your inner spirit, interacting with the world utilizing peace and love.

Prioritize your thoughts. Foremost, try to be the best form of you there is. What does that look like?

Reflection

Understanding Pain

"Pain has a way of clipping our wings and keeping us from being able to fly, and if left unresolved you, can almost forget that you were ever created to fly in the first place."

We would not be human if we had never experienced pain. Pain has an insidious way of permeating our very essence and becoming part of who we are; broken, patched, incomplete.

If we learn to compartmentalize pain, acknowledge it, but not allow it to consume us, we will, indeed, fly. The difficult part is to be consistent, positive, and action-oriented.

Each log on this cabin has been strategically placed. Any rotten or unusable ones have been tossed, so the integrity of this shack is sustained.

Humans cannot escape life without experiencing pain. We all have it both emotionally and physically. I heard someone say once, "If you don't have pain, you won't appreciate the state of well being." That resonates with me, so when I am sick, I try to remember the aches, the pains, and the inconveniences, so that when I am healthy, I can proclaim, "I am so happy I am not in pain!" Enjoy the times and days when you have no pain, but expect that pain will return to visit. We have the opportunity to choose our pain. We can decide what will hurt us emotionally. Some of us allow more pain in than is necessary.

Think of a recent or past pain that you still allow to actively rule your emotions. Acknowledge it did exist, but then realize holding on to it merely hurts your soul, your spirit. Gradually, redirect your mind to more positive experiences. In time, you will escape the pain of that moment.

Reflection

Moral Support

In Paul's story, Mack doesn't enlist the help of his friends and family in dealing with his searching for answers. He relies on himself. That could have been dangerous for who knows what he could have encountered when he returned to the shack? Perhaps the murderer or some deranged person intent on doing him harm.

When we initiate a long journey to understanding life, we need the support of others. If we try to do it alone, it may not turn out as successfully as Mack's journey.

GPS may not get us there. There may be no roads leading to our inner shack. So how can we achieve a successful journey?

When I first used a GPS, I was going to my future daughter-in-law's wedding shower alone in a nearby city. It was in the hills and I had never been there. My GPS had me going on this windy, scary road around the mountain. I fear heights and hate driving alone anyway, but I still kept going. When I finally got there a good thirty minutes late, folks laughed and told me there was a highway on the other side of the house. I just came the back way! I learned GPS doesn't always do its job.

Had I asked folks how to get there, I could have saved time and stress by driving on a highway instead of dirt roads!

Gathering all our bounty, we will see that others may have journeyed to the same place and their words might show us the way. Gather your humility and listen to the words of wise ones in your life.

On this page, draw someone present or past in your life you deem wise. Why is that person the one you chose? How has that person helped you or how do you believe s/he is able to help you now?

Reflection

Fear of the Unknown

"So, why do I have so much fear in my life?"

"Because you don't believe. You don't know that we love you. The person who lives by his fears will not find freedom in my love. I am not talking about rational fears regarding legitimate dangers, but imagined fears, and especially the projection of those into the future. To the degree that those fears have a place in your life, you neither believe that I am good nor know deep in your heart that I love you. You sing about it, you talk about it, but you don't know it."

I don't know about you, but it is very difficult for me to maintain faith and believing in a God I cannot see. I cannot hear him clearly. I spend my days praying for a stronger faith and I fear when I have none or have very little faith.

Many of us are in the same boat. We want to believe, but somehow we are not blessed with a total acceptance in our soul. So are we going to hell because of our doubts?

I had a wonderful spiritual advisor who left this earth way too early. Father George Wolf understood my conflicted spirit and by maintaining regular communication with him, I was able to discern that everyone doubts. He referred me to Mother Teresa's writings. If that great woman doubted, then, I am indeed in good company. He continually reminded me that God knows what is in my heart.

We can't live our lives in fear. We can't live in despair. We must find hope and we must find love. It doesn't happen to us in our sleep (although some people have reported dreams that changed their lives). We must actively search for truths. I believe the first step is to love.

I fell in love with shacks after reading **The Shack**. Everywhere I found one, I would be reminded of the truisms embodied within the shack and I would sense a calm overcome my spirit and love surround me. What is your favorite shack?

Even though the cold and austerity surround this shack, within it I imagine warmth, light, and safety.

Draw your perfect shack. What amenities would it contain?

Reflection

In the Moment

Frequently we hear folks admonish us that we'd better "live in the moment." For sure, those who live in the past and those who live solely in the future, those folks certainly aren't able to celebrate the moment in which they are truly alive. We cannot change the past or really impact the future completely, but we can darn well regulate what we are doing today. So when clouds surround our thoughts and threaten to bring us down, we can learn to not listen to that negativity. It sounds easy enough, but it is very difficult work.

First we must find solace in the fact that we are safe, good, and loved. I teach that to my high school students. It is a mantra they must hear over and over until it sinks in. It is amazing to me to see the changes in the attitudes of children who were angry, stressed, and out of control. After a few doses of that mantra, their lives began to unfold into beautiful and fruitful ones. You don't have to take my word for it. Just try it. Every time you think a negative thought, close your eyes, count to 10, and then think of at least two positive thoughts.

Think you can't do it? Ask someone to help you. Ask them to give you two positives. Then repeat as necessary. Every time you think a negative thought, acknowledge the thought, then let positivity surround it. Whether you believe it or not, we are a part of a living universe. Our God, our supreme being, the force of the universe will give us what we ask for. If we embrace negativity, that will define us. If we embrace positivity, that will become who we are.

Remember Mack worrying and filling his soul with negativity? What happened when he entered the shack of life? His entire life changed.

Your life can change as well, but the invitation cannot remain in your pocket, on your dresser, or on the kitchen table. It MUST be responded to in kind. You must make the effort to eradicate negativity in your life. No one can do it for you.

As a therapist, I see many folks who want some magic to create happiness for them. If the therapist can dispense a pill, or a mantra, then they expect happiness. This will not happen unless the person or you actually do something. You must practice the tools you were given.

On the next page, draw your head. Fill in with either pictures or words all that is going on right now with you. Color the negative ones red and the positive ones green. The neutral ones can be colored blue. After this exercise, look at how many red ones there are. Do they take over your mind? If so, it is time to start thinking positivity and it is not easy.

Reflection

Loneliness

What is it about a person who can be surrounded by others and still feel lonely? What does it mean to be lonely? Perhaps loneliness can be described as an isolated feeling. A person is isolated emotionally, mentally, and spiritually. That does not mean others are not around that person. It's as if the coldness of the world surrounds that person and s/he feels a great sadness because of it.

Surely a road exists somewhere in this picture. Perhaps it is to the right of the shack. Or not. But we really do not know. Only the person(s) living there know the truth. We outsiders can only guess. We can think, oh, you poor soul! You need a neighbor close by! Perhaps someone can come visit you. That will solve the problem.

The only one who can help an individual immersed in loneliness and sadness is that person him/herself. Others can share strategies, but that lonely person must do the work. Others cannot do it for him/her.

Wouldn't it be lovely to just purchase a happy pill with no consequences? Note I said "consequences." There are pills to which people reach when they are sad and/or lonely. Those include drugs, both legal and otherwise, alcohol, and risky behaviors of all sorts. These remedies are only temporary fixes and bring with them all sorts of related problems and hazards.

The simple thing is to start educating yourself about life. What are your goals? What do you want from life? How do you want to reach those goals? And, most importantly, what work are you prepared to do in order to achieve those goals?

Yes, you can have moral supporters, but, in the end, it's all about you and what you input into your life. *On the next page, map out your goals – times, deadlines, ways to get there, etc. Deep breath, relax, and put some great music on while you do so.*

Mack knew he could not bring his friends or family on the journey to the shack. He needed to make a solo trip.

Reflection

Comparing

Mack didn't compare himself to others. All he knew is that he was forlorn and in a bad place. He was even beyond that part where we wish we were someone else.

Look around you and see how others are faring. I am ashamed to admit it, but when I used to meet friends from years gone by, I was almost always secretly thrilled that the woman was fatter than I or had more wrinkles. I've also envied others who proclaimed loudly, "I am a millionaire." Grimace.

Fast forward to now. I realize material things do not a happy person make. Yes, we need comfort, heat, and shelter. But not excess. That is sadly what our culture espouses – you need more no matter what. Turn off the ads. Take stock of what you really need. I am still in the process of minimalizing. I do not think I will ever get there, but I will continue working on it. I do know that I do not care what my friends or neighbors have. They can have better cars, homes, beach houses, and money in the bank. I do not care.

What I do care about is that I have friends and family whom I love and who reciprocate with care and love. I have time to enjoy their company and no amount of money can ever purchase that. So, like the little shack in between the two larger homes, smile for all that you are and all that you will be.

The uniqueness of the small shack surrounded by larger buildings should not take away from the utility of the little shack. It does not lessen its intent – to shelter.

It all depends on what is going on in your inner shack. That buff guy playing football looks pretty good, as does the female CEO pulling in millions of dollars. But are they as happy as you or even happier than you? You never know what their inner sanctum looks or feels like.

Stop comparing. Just look at how you can live your life and then do so with all your might. Let's face it. Only you can live your life and you cannot live it through others. Simple.

Below use some of your favorite colors and just scribble. Close your eyes and fill the page. Take your time. Don't try for realism. Just create lines that are straight or curvy. Enjoy the experience. You are getting it! You are learning to enjoy you.

Reflection

Darkness

Sometimes it feels as if the darkness will never lift. The clouds cover all that is around us and we cannot appreciate the lively colors and beauty that surround us. When these dark feelings take over our body, what are we to do?

We are not sure what's within, but we do feel that eerie darkness that threatens to envelop us were we to step into that yard. But the darkness so far on this earth is not never-ending. Darkness gives way to light, albeit sometimes not very much.

I once met a teacher from Yellow Knife, Canada. I have never been there, but can share with you what she told me. She said that people get stir crazy after a while of having six months or more of darkness. Little kids go outside and play during the day and it is dark. Certainly not light! They get used to it, but after a while, even the teachers have to leave to see the light in order to return to work in the darkness.

The darkness itself is not bad. It's just the quantity that makes it unbearable. Some brave souls can take more of the darkness than others. Those who are not able to, need to seek relief from the darkness.

They may find relief temporarily and then lapse back into the grips of darkness. Then they will need visits to their therapist or physician or mentor in order to balance out the darkness.

Just like yin and yang, we need a balance of spirituality, emotions, name it what you will, we need balance.

Reflections

Dark combined with light equals wholeness. What are your dark thoughts? Draw them below.

Turmoil

Sometimes it feels as if a tornado is overtaking our mind. Our thoughts become so jumbled that our words tumble out incoherently. We don't even recognize the trouble we are in for.

We hear the rumbling and feel the pain that is to come, but we don't know what to do. Our inner shack has no meteorologist to tell us to go and hide. We need to seek assistance before the eye of the storm passes us.

Who works as your mentor? Who helps you sort out feelings and thoughts? Everyone needs someone he or she trusts and respects. Find that person and be sure to check in regularly with him/her.

When the storm finally hits, you will have strategies in place.
- Know the signs of the storm. These are called your triggers. What makes you start to become unglued?
- Practice with your therapist/mentor how not to react to these thoughts. I am deathly afraid of birds (don't tell my students) and if one landed on me, I am sure I would have a heart attack). So that is a trigger. How can I make sure I won't overreact?
- By practicing! Yes, we have a word we use in therapy called desensitization. That means I should look at photos of beautiful birds. Smile. Make that a pleasant experience.
- Gradually get nearer to the offending thought. So, place your head in that same room with that nasty girl who always hurts your feelings. Look at her in your mind's eye. Smile. Even if she is sticking her tongue out at you. It's not real. It's just a thought.
- Remember that you cannot control anyone but yourself. You CAN control your feelings.
- Practice

Below write out what triggers your anger/strong emotions. Then make a plan to keep those thoughts in check. You do not have to react to them. This is hard, folks. It takes a lot of work, but you are worth it and you can do it!

Reflection

Isolation and Desolation

The Shack was certainly a place of desolation, degradation, and intense pain at first glance. But when Mack reaches it by himself under providential guidance, he finds that even an ugly horrific place can have some redeeming qualities. It can even help you find out things about yourself that will enhance the quality of your life.

A woman I know woke up one New Year's Day shaking from the agony of a dream she had the night before. While others were revelling and kissing their loved ones, she was mute. Listening to others. Observing others. And once fast asleep in her bed, she experienced a running review of her marriage courtroom style. The scene was not pleasant. She did not know why she was in the courtroom, but accusations began to fly.

She relived some very sad moments in her life. When she awoke before the rest of the family, she lay in bed wondering what had brought all that pain to the surface. She had thought she had forgiven and put all the anguish aside. But this morning it was raw.

How would she deal with this intensity? Would she shove it back down to her subconscious, this time sealing it once more? Or was there a way for her to deal with the pain she thought she could control?

With others making New Year's resolutions, here she was experiencing a path through the past that not only made her sad, but as she was grieving, she thought of all the hurt that would ensue should she dare to speak of those past wrongs.

Much as the isolated shack above, life sometimes seems bereft. No sign of life appears on the scene. But who knows what is inside? Only you.

So what do you do when pain surfaces and you do not know what to do with this pain? This is a signal – a sure signal – that you need professional help maybe for just a little while, but maybe for a very, very long time.

Did you know that even therapists have personal counselors as well? Most of us aren't immune to negativity and need some help in assigning it its proper place. Filling up the shack above with more negativity – garbage, filth, hurts, and more. Well, it could just rot or maybe explode if not properly taken care of as it should.

This is something you probably should not try to handle alone. There is no stigma seeking help when the universe sends you an alarming signal, even if it is in a dream.

Reflection

What fears do you have? Are they reality based? Are they imagined? Draw them below.

Freedom

When Mack finally met his demons head on, he was able to free himself from the spasms of misery clutching his heart and mind.

Most birds were created to fly. Being grounded for them is a limitation within their ability to fly, not the other way around. You, on the other hand, were created to be loved. So for you to live as if you were unloved is a limitation, not the other way around. Pain has a way of clipping our wings and keeping us from being able to fly. If unresolved for very long, you can almost forget you were ever created to fly in the first place.

Those are powerful words to Mack from Papa. In case you forgot, Papa is the personification of God the Father as Christians refer to him. Even if you are not Christian or religious, this is still powerful rhetoric that should stir your soul into action. We are meant to be happy – to fly – to be loved. When we do not feel that love or that ability to sail through the winds of life, then we are swindled out of our very human birthright.

When negativity strikes, reciprocate with a zeal of positive confidence. It is not an easy thing as I have said before. It is far easier to wallow in bitterness than it is to dismiss it and replace it with actions and thoughts that uplift the spirit.

Just accepting what happens without being proactive keeps us in the quagmire of despair and totally enslaved to our emotions. Freedom comes from recognizing truths, but not allowing them to create dissidence within us. We can only control our own reactions and emotions. We cannot control others.

The path to our inner shack may be steep and difficult, but once inside we can make a difference. We can decide what is important within our souls and we can clean out the cobwebs of incidents that are no longer pertinent to our growth.

On the next page, on one side, draw or cut out magazine pictures or even clip art of things that could be your nemesis, your dark side. Look at each one. Acknowledge it. Then repeat to yourself: **This does not define me. I do not have to react negatively. It happened. It is over. I must just let it go.**

For example, if you are still mad at a friend for ignoring you at a party. I mean, this was no ordinary ignoring scenario. This person acted as if you weren't alive. You were so hurt. Devastated. But now it is over. So take a few deep, cleansing breaths and let it go. You cannot change what happened, so why let it affect you now? Forgive that person. Get on with life.

Conscience

Many religious people perform a ritual some call an examination of conscience. This means that they take a toll of what they have done that is good and what they have done that is not so good. They evaluate their life. Some folks do this on a regular basis. Others have never even heard, much less tried it. But for those who do, their mental health appears to be more fruitful and joyous.

Some folks combine this examination of consciousness with a prayer.

Conscience is like our moral muscle. The more we use it, the more it grows. The development of conscience often comes with age, but it's possible for an 18 year-old to have a more developed conscience than a 40 year-old.

If we overuse our conscience, just as one might do to a muscle, the world might seem very overwhelming. You spend all this time trying to make sense of the world and it comes crashing down on that person because no one can do everything right from one moment on. When the crash comes, such a person often then discards conscience altogether, often thinking it doesn't pay to work so hard to be good. Mack continually sought to understand what he should have or could have done in the past in order to change his dire circumstances.

Do an examination of conscience. What things are you doing right in your life? What could you do better?

Reflection

Procrastination

I'm not even sure how to begin writing this section in this blog. I have almost completed half of the book I am now naming **Shack Blessings**. It's not a collection of cards, but a rambling collection of thoughts about how the book *The Shack* influenced my life, with my experience as a therapist. An art therapist to be exact. But something is holding me back. What evil thoughts lurk in the back of my mind as I attempt to finish this book? I was given permission by the author of *The Shack* several years ago to come on this journey. Why am I afraid? Aren't we all like that at times? We start something and half way through it are sure we don't want to finish it, or just don't.

Like this shack that someone constructed and abandoned. Or is someone still working on it? Is it cared for and loved? Does anyone ever stay there?

We really do not know. We only see an edifice with overgrown weeds and some evidence of pruning around the base. Has it lost its usefulness?

How do we know that the creator of this small shack is not trying to ready it for a summertime spot?

Same for my writings. Perhaps I am writing in my head and some day it will be evident for all to see. Perhaps. Maybe not.

I am not even sure. All I am sure of is that there is this burning desire to keep this small piece of written work and finalize it someday. When that day will come, I am not sure. But I have not given up. I am finished procrastinating. I will try to write one entry each day for the next month.

I'll check back next month - July 18 and will honestly share if I have written at least 20 entries. Why don't you pick up something you have been procrastinating about doing and make a plan?

I double dare you! Much later...yes, I did work on the book some more, although not regularly. This book has taken me much longer than other writing I have done. I do not know why since it is something I really feel strongly about.

Below draw something you have procrastinated about. Then on the next page, write or draw a plan to make sure you finish this project, paper, or deed you need to do.

Reflection

Storms

Today a young teen drowned. One day happy, enjoying summer and the lake, and the next – gone forever. The pain his family and friends are feeling is unimaginable, but this could happen to any of us at any time.

Sometimes we are so caught up in our own lives we fail to see the misery around. We are blind to other people's pain. But then nature takes its course and we are all blended together in recognizing that all we really have is each other. We are not alone in this journey. We are social, sentient beings who need one another.

We may think we are so alone in the storm, hiding in our edifice with four walls and a ceiling. We are insulated from the world, or so we think. We need to leave this cabin from time to time to replenish our supplies, and what will we see out there?

Will the storm ravage the land and leave in its wake nothing but destruction?

What storms have you had in your lives? How have you coped?
On the next page, draw those storms and write or draw how you have dealt with them. Share these comments and drawings with someone near to you. How has this person overcome adversity in their own lives?

In addition to drawing and describing your storms, why not draw additional humans who are there for you, or those who could be there for you in case you need them.

Don't stop at just thinking about it – go call or visit someone on this list. Let that person know you depend on them and want that person to be able to depend on you. Go, do it now! Don't wait until the last minute. We need each other so badly. When was the last time you told that person you need him or her? When was the last time you reached out to anyone?

In **The Shack**, we hear Jesus saying, *"All I want from you is to trust me with what little you can, and grow in loving people around you with the same love I share with you. It's not your job to change them, or to convince them. You are free to love without an agenda."*

So, go find someone to love again. Reach out and hold that person near to your heart. It doesn't matter why it has been a long time. Just love and let others know you are there for them, just like you hope they are there for you. Do it now. Don't wait until the storm hits.

Reflection

Living in the Moment

Just when you think you are so totally alone, you take a minute out of your miserable pity party and notice something. The storm that has been raging seems calmer. As you peer out the window, you notice that the sky is a beautiful shade of purple, with yellow tinges within the streaks of lavender.

You notice that further down the road is another abode. A place where someone else might be watching the same storm. You take a deep breath and realize you are not alone. You, and many others, are looking at the same sky, having the same thoughts perhaps.

You note the beauty of the hills, the trees, and the vegetation. You take another deep breath and notice the varying shades of green. How can there be so many? Your soul feels calm. You realize that this is a good way to live.

Some folks call it "living in the moment." Whatever it is called, thinking positive thoughts creates harmony within and that same harmony allows us to lead a happier and more joyous life.

When was the last time you noticed your breathing? Most of us breathe in a shallow manner. We cannot seem to get enough air. But practice deep breathing.

Put your hand on your stomach. Notice your hand going up and down. Inhale deeply. Don't elevate your shoulders. Let the air come in from your abdomen.

Hold that air for a few seconds and exhale through your mouth. Imagine all the positive coming in and allowing the negative to be released.

Try that for a few times. Just think about breathing. Now does that make sense when you are exercising and the coach reminds you to breathe? Sometimes when we are stressed we take those inadequate shallow breaths and we have to work too hard to just breathe.

Practicing deep breathing allows us to cleanse our bodies with fresh, pure oxygen and then releasing it slowly, allows us to start to delete negativity from our lives. Practice with a friend or relative. Try it now. How do you feel?

On this page, write how you feel about deep breathing. Maybe you will draw someone deep breathing. I hope that someone is YOU!

Reflection

Life Isn't Always Gray

Sometimes we feel comforted by the grayness of the ocean – the starkness of the land, and the cold winds that blow upon us as we view the waves. Those waves come close, but we really do not expect them to flow over the deck and into our hearth.

Similar to the ocean close to the cabin above, so, too, are the waters of our life. They lap up close to us, threatening us at times, and soothing us at other times. Our conflict is finding the time to just relax, be in the moment, and enjoy the ocean no matter what its force.

Snuggling deep down inside the cabin, perhaps covered with a blanket or two, we can hear the pounding of the waves upon the rocks. We can hear the lapping of the water near the cabin, but we are safe.

We are safe. We repeat that mantra many times in our day just so we can truly believe it. Yes, we are safe. The world is good and there are many good things in this world.

To think otherwise is folly. It would be as if we were inviting evil into our lives. How can we be so naïve as to think the world is good?

One thing we must learn is that we must control only what we can control. We cannot control others. We can only control how we perceive the actions or words of others. We can choose to make a positive slant on such actions or words, or we can choose to allow ourselves to feel the negativity. Yes, it is a choice.

Most of us do not realize we have this choice. It is very freeing to finally understand the power we have within. It is comparable to the power of the ocean. We can lull ourselves to sleep with positivity. We can enjoy the rhythm of positivity in our lives. If only we make that conscious choice.

Mack had a choice. He could choose to find out more about the letter and return to the shack. He could stay at home. No one would force him or expect him to go. But he went anyway. He made the decision – he made a positive decision for his life.

What decisions have you been putting off? What waves or ripples of disquiet unravel your life's balance? Face those and allow yourself to enter into those thoughts with positivity as an end result.

On this page, draw what is in your ocean of thoughts. How can you make them reveal a good thing in your life?

Reflection

Fences Make Good Neighbors

Sometimes we want to just insulate ourselves from the world. We want to climb into a warm nest and stay there, unfettered by worldly problems.

One way to escape is to give in to your inner guide. You know what makes you happy and you equally know what does not make you happy. You are the boss of your choices. You decide whether something is going to make you content or not.

We can't always be happy. Nice, but not a probability; however, we can create an ambiance within us that makes us less likely to stress out, become sick, or simply to allow the ugly head of negativity to represent us.

Many clients ask me how to do that seemingly impossible act of choosing to not let things bother them. This is when I share another book that has been useful in my life. It is ***"The Four Agreements"*** by Don Miguel Ruiz. Ruiz's family are comprised of shamans who passed down wisdom from generation to generation. I have read and reread the book many times.

The four agreements are simple:
- Do your personal best.
- Have integrity.
- Don't make assumptions.
- Don't take things personally.

Wow! Can you imagine doing the third and fourth agreement? These tenets are so difficult to actualize in daily life. We all make assumptions and take things personally. That's just what we do.

But, the secret is out: we do not have to do those things! We can change. Yes, it is very difficult. It takes practice. We are changing bad habits – old habits – hard habits to break. We are replacing them with new thoughts. I would never lead you astray. It is difficult. But even Mack in the shack decided he would be open to what was to come.

He fought taking things personally and was able to cement a friendship with the Trinity. While we may not have that exceptional experience, we surely can learn that we have to open our hearts and minds. We need to realize that when others do things we deem hurtful, perhaps they are suffering as well. Let it go! Create a positive twist on life incidents.

What can you let go? How can you open your life to love, positivity, and less stress?

Reflection

Counting our Blessings

Sometimes I think we just forget how good we have it. Recently, I heard someone complaining about the, yes, believe it, the **HORRORS** of remodeling their home. They were inconvenienced by the painter who had to continually reschedule his services. Oh, my, what are we all about in Western society?

I woke up today, had food, shelter, and a day off. I could do what I wanted, when I wanted, and where I wanted. I should have no complaints.

My plate is full and I should acknowledge those blessings before I complain. Complaining is a habit. Sometimes we do not even know we are doing it. We just complain because that is what we have always done.

Now some of us have family who will remind us, sometimes not too gently, however, that we need to be grateful for our lives. Others of us are tolerated by our fellow human beings and labeled as grumpy, pain in the "you know what," and so on. It does not have to be that way. We do not have to be complainers. We can change our habit of negativity. It is certainly not easy.

Changing a habit requires much effort. Those of you who forget to floss each and every day know what I mean. If it was never a habit from childhood, it is most difficult to make into a habit in adulthood. It can be done, though.

Every day is a new day. Stop lamenting the past. You can't change it, but you certainly can learn from it. Stop the negative thoughts. Just do it.

For example, you wake up, and the first thing you think about is the ache in your knees. First, be thankful for waking up at all. Look around and find two things for which you are grateful. It could be the sun shining in through the window. It could be for a comfortable sleeping accommodation. It could be for the air you breathe.

Seriously, each and every one of us have things to be grateful for and positive thoughts we can think about. Challenge yourself. Whenever dark thoughts lurk in your mind, counter them with multiple positive thoughts.

Reflection

Chaos

Some of us are terrified lately. We are terrified by terrorism. We are terrified by protestors at rallies. We are terrified by weather and threats of annihilation of our very species. That is why I have stopped watching the news *all the time*. You do know news is streamed throughout the day on many channels, and most of it is the bad, the ugly, and the terrible news of the day. All the great things that happened aren't highlighted. The headlines are enough to give one heart failure.

It would be nice to have an isolated place no one knows about and just go there and hide out for a while, inviting in only light and warmth. We have allowed the thistles and thorns to grow within us and then we complain of the pain and heartache.

We can do something about it. We can shed those thoughts that bring us unhappiness. We can decide which things are within our control. If they are not (and who is to say they are or aren't?), then decide today that you won't let your spirits down because of those thoughts. You are in charge. You definitely can decide to choose happiness.

I had an old friend who endured torture and cruelty while imprisoned in Romania during the Communist takeover in the early 1940's. All the intellectuals who could be found were gathered together and thrown naked into a small enclosure. There was no room to lie down, except a small place where one person could lie down. They took turns sleeping. Those men were imprisoned over a month and they survived. How in the world is that possible?

Well, this kind old man said that each professional would teach the others about his work. He learned about dentistry, accounting, and law – all through lectures delivered by imprisoned men. They all assumed an attitude of survival rather than victimization. He lived many years after that experience and wrote a book about his experience.

Another thing I learned from this wonderful man is that he loved our country. He loved our idea of democracy. He knew what socialism would bring. So, today, I decide I will be happy, even though there are negative things going on. I will reflect on the joys and blessings I have and accept that I am in charge. What a wonderful feeling to decide to be happy.

What is the chaos in your life? Can you simplify the problem? Draw or write here what is heavy on your mind.

Reflection

Task Completion

We attended a friend's son's wedding and someone was circulating a book entitled *A Bible for Women of Color*. We were supposed to find a verse as a guide to this new young bride and highlight it as a message of hope and encouragement for her.

I looked through it and found it difficult to find a passage quickly enough that would be fruitful advice. I did not have all day to do so. I finally found something, although it was not what I really wanted, but highlighted the part anyway.

Many times we have a task set before us that we feel is too difficult or we feel ambivalent about the tools we have to adequately complete the task. So what are our coping mechanisms we use in order to thwart negativity or noncompliance?

It's just like a worn, dilapidated shack. What would you do in order to restore it adequately so someone could visit there? Just looking at its façade, I'd say it was almost impossible to do a quick renovation.

But to the seasoned builder, he could see possibilities. He could see shortcuts that we would not begin to understand. So it is with our lives. When we have tasks to complete, sometimes we don't know where to begin.

In order to create a whole vision of our task in life, we need to take baby steps. We need to think of one thing we can do to improve our lives. In this shack, we could possibly think of removing the roof and replacing it. That would be one thing. It is only through actually beginning and visualizing the end that we can truly move forward.

If our problem is that we believe our children don't visit us enough, we need to strategize how to solve that problem. Perhaps the first thing to do is to see if that is even a problem. As we age, our life's mortality becomes more evident, and we begin to cling to things, to people, to the way things were or should be, in our opinion.

It's time to look at our problems objectively. Truly, there are two sides to each problem. Try looking at a problem from another perspective. When you are young and building a family, time is precious. So much time is spent on creating a safe environment for the family and that takes a job outside of the house. It takes time to keep the house serviceable for the growing family. The list goes on. Why, those young people probably think they see enough of their parents. So whose problem is it? Probably the parents. They need to stop thinking of their wishes and demands and think of the younger ones and their needs as well.

We all have situations that bother us, but learning to look at a problem from a different perspective usually helps build understanding. Once we understand a problem and turn it into a non-problem or a neutral situation, we can truly say, "*It is what it is,*" and we can proceed through life without all those hurt feelings, those sad memories, and those unreasonable demands.

When we are able to think logically, reasonably, and take our time in doing so, the quality of our lives will definitely improve. Imagine looking at a beautiful piece of art – describe the colors, the lines, and its design. Take a deep breath as you do so. Focus on the painting or sculpture. You are being in the moment. This is what we have – the present.

We cannot change the past and we cannot create the future – all we do have is the present. Take a moment and look at something in your home or office. I mean really look at it. I like to take a jelly bean or a piece of candy for this activity. Use all your senses in experiencing the flavor, the color, the texture outside of your mouth. Then put it in your mouth and continue experiencing the taste, the texture, and the aroma. Take a deep breath. **You are being in the moment!**

Reflection

Family Change

Family dynamics change when additional members are added to the mix or taken out of the mix. Divorce, death, or separation influence the dynamics of a family. When children marry, new in-laws come into the fold. When children are born, the hierarchy of the family changes. Sometimes this change is very good and sometimes this change can be very devastating to some or all of the family members.

Dark clouds can accumulate and wash away some of the very grit the family is made of and members who are often not forewarned are caught unaware. As members of such families, we do have choices. We can, first of all, just be aware that change will and has happened. Our family is growing and morphing into a new family. We can fight it or we can simply acknowledge that we cannot change it. With this type of attitude, we begin to see that we do not have to allow the changes to undo our souls. If the change is creating havoc, perhaps a prayer or kind thought for those whom we think are causing the unrest will keep our spirits calm.

Each family has its unique characteristics. New members, excluding children, who by their nature, cannot be held responsible for creating a new and harmonious relationship with the former family; however, adults can be held to this standard. They can realize things are different in their new situation and act accordingly. Judge less. Interfere less. Finally, the new member can attempt to think positively about the new family.

The former family dynamics will change as well. Those individuals would do best to accept that the newbies are what they are. Rarely is change going to occur, and, if it does at all, it will be a slow process.

Guidelines for the family infused with new blood is to welcome all, think only positively, and accept. Only then will the family structure remain strong and intact. Taking things personally or making assumptions only leads to increased stress and depression.

Take a deep breath. Think of your family and/or members who seem to create havoc. Say a prayer for that person(s) and forgive them. You will finally feel released from that pressure of guilt, anger, and forgiveness. This is for you.

Reflection

Tumultuous Times

I remember as a child avoiding cracks on the sidewalk because I had heard a jingle saying something like, *step on a crack, break your mother's back*. It wasn't just a child's game to me. It somehow permeated my mind and threatened my very sense of security. I would not step on that crack even if part of me said it was just a saying. I had too much love, devotion, and need of my mother. No way was I going to ever jeopardize her life or wellbeing.

In this day and age, some of us are sent social media messages that threaten us with the most benign message that we won't love someone/thing the media is touting if we don't repost, retweet, or reply to the message. So, if you love Jesus, you must repost to prove that you do.

Seriously? Deep breath here. These are the things that intervene in the serenity of my days. You must be thinking *Boy, does she ever have issues*. So, good for you! It doesn't bother you, but I can honestly reveal many people feel the same way as I. In their inner depths they think that just maybe those dire warnings or threats might come true. So, what is the problem with complying?

That line of thinking is what can get us into serious trouble. For instance, everything we post or say goes on and on for perpetuity, I have been told. It's like taking a tube of toothpaste, removing all the paste, and then trying to insert it all back into the tube. Without some astute resources, that would be an impossibility. Same with comments, written or oral. Once said, they are out in the universe.

What do those two thoughts have to do with one another? For one, fear is contagious. You feel a bit of fear with the request to repost something. Even if you believe in Jesus and don't repost, what does that prove? But part of you is feeling a bit of stress. Add that to the stress that the car in front of you swerved and almost caused you to hit it and you have a recipe for increased and improved stress.

When one experiences stress, what does one do? Some of us yell obscenities. Our brains go into fight or flight mode. We are ramped up. Our blood pressure rises. We might yell at the next human we see or animal. It's collective. One thing leads to another. Being aware of these tricks in our minds, we can control them and not allow them to invade and capture our minds.

Our thinking minds really can think if we take the time to learn strategies how to do so. First thing is to acknowledge those stressors. Yes, I despise requests to share benign requests. So, I posted that I don't want to repost things that I already know unless they are of interest to my 500+ friends and family on Facebook. You wouldn't sit down at a party and tell the person next to you, *if you believe in Jesus, tell the whole gang*! That would not make sense. Unless, perhaps you were at a revival.

Take charge of your life and your thinking. Don't allow others to influence who or what you are. Finally, do not be afraid. *On the next page, write some things that stress you out and ways you can face those stressors, or better yet, eliminate them.*

Papa is watching out for you!

Reflection

Hidden

You would never suspect that I, as a therapist, suffer daily from anxiety and depression – that I have to consciously utilize strategies I've learned in order to make it through the day without major drama. That is the hidden part of my personality and my life.

Although a part of me is hidden, it still is an integral part of my personality and persona. Yes, it exists. Sometimes it is easier to spot than others. Just like the shack above, when the day is clear, more can be seen. It is surely still in existence.

I can create elaborate facades to keep it secluded, but there is no denying it is. The hay, fences, vegetation, and fog can disguise this shack, but it cannot make it disappear totally.

For those of us who battle mental illnesses on a daily basis, it is a fact that we will always have to live with these impediments. We can surely learn to live with them, so these infirmities are assets.

How else would I be able to understand the deeply angry teen had I not walked in his shoes?

How else would I be able to understand the woman who sees no hope in her life and feels sucked in as a victim with every relationship she holds near to her?

The list is endless, but the possibilities surpass the probabilities. Yes, we can learn to live with our inadequacies. At times we wish them to be secret, but at other times, we can allow them to be on front stage, allowing others to learn and understand from our experience with them.

Our life's journey is relatively short, so one important thing I have learned is to make sure that I am always enjoying or learning from a moment. True, not every moment can be peaceful and/or powerful, but each moment can be joyful in the fact that we learn from arduous moments, from difficult decisions, from troubling conflicts....

Our society and, Western culture in particular, has created a scenario in our minds where mental illness or troubles are bad things – things we need to be ashamed of and hide. In recent years many individuals and groups have toiled endlessly to eradicate the stigma of mental illness. We are all crazy, but in various dimensions and strengths.

Take a moment to look within your soul. What are your weaknesses? Your problems? Your traits that keep you from becoming the person you wish to be? Then re-examine those issues with a positive lens – a rose colored lens, if you will.

What can you do to keep those issues from becoming you? How are you able to deal with them on a daily basis? One question I always remind my clients of is, Am I able to control this? If I am not able to control this, I surely am able to control how I react to it. I choose positivity. I will not allow my emotions to derail my attitude. I will not allow others to dictate how I feel. I am totally capable of choosing myself. And I choose positive thoughts.

Yes, it is extremely difficult to do so, but it can be done. It just takes practice. A lot of practice. You have taken decades to be who you are now. To change the way you fundamentally think will also take increased practice and that does not happen in a month. Or two. Or three. Maybe in six months you will be able to notice change, but only if you are vigilant and continue to practice positivity and light.

Take a deep breath. What can you control? Who can you control?

Release that breath slowly. Close your eyes and utter a phrase of positivity: *I can do it. I am safe. I am good. I am loved.*

On the next page, draw your issues. Surround them with positive clouds. Play some soothing music and enjoy life.

Reflection

Losing My Religion

It's not something to be proud of or something we just share with anyone, but losing one's religion is not only part of an old hit, it's also the sad feeling that many of us experience as we mature and become disillusioned by churches and church teachings.

Connecting with others who experience familiar feelings allows us to learn to grapple with what is important to each of us. I have heard many a time the term "Cafeteria Catholics." They are supposedly those individuals who decide which doctrines to believe and which to discard. But who is the judge? I've heard priests say that premarital sex is not wrong and I've also heard from others that it is. Who is telling the truth? What does the Bible say? And, for that matter, how can one even possibly begin to believe that some writings are infallible works of God when they were written by men?

It's too difficult in one chapter to begin to delineate the errors of organized religion. One true thing is that there is a god. He or she or it. Some folks believe that Jesus was sent to us to help us out. Others believe in other deities. What feels important at this point is to learn the truths for you and to stand by them.

Surely, there are others who feel the same. I am not advocating for one religion over another, but what I am advocating for is that we stop and educate ourselves and prioritize our beliefs. Perhaps then we will begin to understand the bigger picture. Perhaps then we will find peace.

Once when I asked a priest to help me with my doubts, he told me to read Mother Teresa's writings. He told me she doubted as well. He added that I was in pretty good company.

That one priest that one time helped me feel better about my nagging doubts about my religion. I know that all we can do is try. We are human and will make mistakes, but it is important to think once in awhile and readjust our minds.

Below write what your spirituality is at this point in life. What is important? What would you care do discard? Write or draw a small prayer.

Reflection

Poor in Spirit

Somewhere I've heard that being poor in spirit is a good thing. What does that actually mean? Like the shack above that is primal to the eye, we see a poverty of sorts, a lack of richness. How does that image resonate with our souls? Should our souls be bereft of richness? And what is that richness whereof we speak? Certainly material riches are not what decorate and manifest the soul, so what then are the characteristics that allow one to be humble in spirit?

This poor in spirit phrase comes from the Dead Sea scrolls. It is not a new thought. Rather ancient. The Western culture idolizes material wealth, physical appearance, and accumulated accolades of varying sorts. How can one be poor in spirit, yet successful in the eyes of Western society?

Or can one be?

Look back at the picture of the shack in this chapter. Even though the shack is apparently unattended, unloved, and abandoned, there is something starkly inviting about the photo. Is it that it is surrounded by blue skies above? Is the ground cover pleasant, although seemingly uncared for as well? The lines and stark contrasts make this a soothing picture to look at for some. For others, it is clear and unassuming.

Take a look inside. An honest appraisal of the real you. Your body is merely a shell that will someday be shed, but the real you will always be. What are your core beliefs? Are you conflicted about who you are? It might be time to start deciding what you stand for and how you will implement that knowledge. *On the next page, write or draw qualities you wish to improve upon or already have instilled within the real you. Yes, there are folks who are simple in this life and have shed the accruements of false imagery. Where do you stand? And for what?*

Reflection

Surrounded by Beauty

Sometimes we are judged by the company we keep. If we are surrounded by beauty and goodness, our entire façade will reflect those qualities. Gazing upon this serene photo, we don't really see that the house is old, in need of repair, and probably not even occupied. What we see is a place of refuge and calm.

Do others receive our aura of goodness? Do we radiate kindness and beauty? We can do so not only by our words, but by our actions as well. When we stoop to the ground to pick up a piece of discarded trash, we signal to others we value cleanliness and orderliness. When we smile at someone on the street, we demonstrate our love of mankind. It is not a difficult task to spread positive vibes in the world. It does not have to cost anything but a few seconds of our time.

Somewhere I read research that said to smile is to increase endorphins in our body that makes us feel happy, even if the smile is forced. What? So if I fake smile, I can really improve my mood?

That sounds ludicrous, but I've practiced it. When I've been in a grouchy or bad mood, I've remembered that little bit of advice, and forced myself to smile. Voila! I am not kidding you. My entire persona relaxed and I felt the negativity dissipate as if by magic.

Our bodies and spirits are amazing. We can do more than we think. Yes, we are in charge of our lives and our perspectives. Who really likes to wallow in despair and darkness?

So the next time you feel a dark cloud encumbering your progress through the day, take a moment and smile. Yes, fake smile. Take a few deep breaths and check out how you feel. You should be feeling yourself evaporate into happiness. Or serenity. Or just a relaxed state.

On the next page, do an experiment! Write or draw some things that have made your smile turn upside down. What makes you sad? Then read each one and try to see the lining in the silver cloud. So, your kids haven't called you lately. You are feeling unloved. Remind yourself that they do love you and think of one positive moment with that certain child. Is that smile returning to your face? Make it happen. You are in charge of your feelings and your life.

Reflection

Holidays

Sometimes the holidays have ways of conjuring up negativity in our souls. When that happens, some of us become Mr. Grinch. Bah, humbug! Holidays are not fun. Do you realize that you do have a choice? You can make the holidays fun. If you don't want fun, you can at least create an aura of love so that those who are around you won't be affected by your foul mood! And, shame on you, for being so selfish – feeling that you need to pronounce to the world your dissatisfaction with it. It's time to do some soul searching.

Notice in the picture above, there are two benches next to one another. Empty benches. Sitting in the cold, gathering snow, solitary. Sometimes we are just like those benches. We stiffly put ourselves out there alone. We are uninviting and just there. What we don't see is that someone next to us is doing the same thing. If we moved the two closer, cleaned them off, what do you suppose might happen?

A tired skier might find refuge in the comfort of one of those benches. Perhaps a bedraggled hiker might find one of them a quiet respite for a moment.

It is times like this that we need to know we are not alone if we do not want to be. We can dust off our negatives and welcome the positives. Perhaps we can join in the fun of skiing or the joy of walking in the snow. Whatever your perspective is, just know that you are in control of it and only you can change it. Moving these benches does not change their façade. Only the thawing of the snow on the benches makes them inviting to others.

We are social beings. Some of us need people interaction more than others. But every single one of us needs some social interaction. To encourage that, one must truly prepare a place that is inviting to others. You really can do it, you know.

When was the last social gathering you attended? Did you have fun? What did you like best about it? *On the next page, write or draw that party and how you felt. Next time you feel abandoned or alone, remember that event. Smile – yes, even fake smile – and you will lift your spirits.*

Reflection

Retreats

I have only been on a few retreats in my life. One of them was about two years ago at a local seminary in Mt. Angel, Oregon. Aptly named, the facility is surrounded by lovely trees, flowers, and flowing gardens and beautifully kept, stately buildings.

The room we were in could be described as stark. A single bed, firm enough, one pillow and a quilt. A writing desk and, best of all, a private bathroom with a shower. Three meals were provided and the most interesting of all – it was a silent retreat. Yes, you guessed it. No talking. Just listening, praying, and relaxing.

At the end of the three days, folks were invited to relax more and speak, if they so wished. The only part I really found difficult was sitting at a communal dinner table and not being able to talk with another human being. The sounds of chewing, swallowing, and spoons clanking on plates almost drove me crazy.

Our society is not designed for such solitude. It was truly an experience. One never knows what will happen when we shut out all media (forgot to mention there were no televisions or radios around). I could have used some music; nevertheless, it was a pleasant experience.

Surprisingly, I realized I need quiet in my life. I've usually surrounded myself with noise – people, television, Pandora. You mention it. Most of my life is not quiet. When we face the quiet, we see who we really are. Are you ready to practice?

When we examine the house above, we see through it. There is nothing to hide what it is. A simple structure that may have one day been a refuge for others. At this point in its existence, it simply is an abandoned, sterile structure. What good is it? Are we nurturing an abandoned, sterile soul within us?

Reflection

Final Thoughts

A Facebook friend found out I was writing a book based on *The Shack*. She wrote to me and shared the following story.

I was sitting in a house church conference, in Salem, Oregon (a conference I just happened to have created, run and pulled together, in my desire to connect people in the community). A man behind me said "Pssst - are you Dena?" I nodded. He turned out to be an online friend - he handed me a book, **The Shack** *in its pre-published form. He told me I had to read it.*

I resisted. "Dude, I don't read fiction, especially not Christian fiction - most of it is horribly written." He insisted. I complied.

I read that book straight through four times... underlining, highlighting, dog-earing and putting all manner of notes in the margins. I told my then-husband, and our neighbors-in-community (and our entire house church), and my family to, "put down everything, including the bible, and READ this!" I insisted. They complied.

I then contacted Paul Young, and told him I was a rabid fan, and that I had about 50 rabidly fanatical folks who had read his book. He asked if he could come down to our home, in Dallas, Oregon, and speak to our house church - that was his first-ever public talk, in my former living room (I then purchased five cases of his self-published book, prior to its release on Amazon, and passed out copies to all the influential leaders I then-knew - all of whom had huge followings of thousands or more, and Paul credited me with making his book turn into a best-seller).

The Shack *was a huge part of my own journey and Paul was a beloved friend. I shall always be grateful for that beautiful catalyst that said, out loud, what my own soul was fiercely whispering.*

~ Dena Lynn

Just when you think you have a unique handle on things, someone arrives on the scene and shares an even earlier story about the same thing. Yes, Dena found what made her whole in life. This is not to say that **The Shack** made me lose my religion – I was already losing it. It actually gave me religion back again.

No longer will I look upon life as a series of acts – good and bad – I will take the time to realize that we are all doing the best we can and sometimes, just sometimes, we need to re-evaluate our priorities and our beliefs.

On the next page, write or draw what you believe. What is important to you and why? Remember to relax and breathe in deeply and exhale. Yes, you are alive and well!

Reflection

And so the end is here, a bittersweet one, but an ending nevertheless. I hope that you have benefited from these sometimes random thoughts evoked by reading **The Shack**. The movie is sure to add an additional layer of thought provoking material for you to digest.

I hope your days are kind and gentle and your nights relaxing and stress free. I urge you to try to live more in the moment, looking about and enjoying nature, beautiful things you surround yourselves with, and sounds that lift your spirits. Get out there and paint! Listen to music. Venture out to an art gallery. Experience a new kind of food. View a genre of movie you never have watched. Help your neighbor with his/her lawn. Bring a cup of soup to someone sick. Be kind. Love yourself and remember that it is not the riches we leave this earth with that are important. It is the legacy of who we were and how we made people feel that will be the most lasting.

If you liked something about this booklet or just want to comment, I'd love to hear from you via **masabitherapist@gmail.com**.

Peace to you, my friends. We are definitely in this together.

LOLA CARLILE

is a writer, art therapist, but, most of all, an educator invested in helping others find their true meaning in life. She lives on the West Coast with her husband and enjoys writing as meditation.

Made in the USA
Middletown, DE
18 January 2022